Escape to Manchuria!

by

Gillian Thornhill

Escape to Manchuria …and thence to the Promised Land!

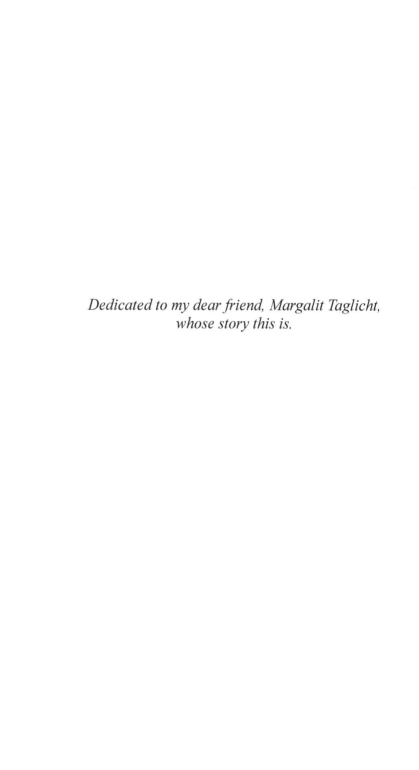

*Dedicated to my dear friend, Margalit Taglicht,
whose story this is.*

Acknowledgements

I would like to thank: Margalit for providing me with detailed memories of the history she lived through. Also her two sons. Rafi Taglicht for help with the content and for organising appropriate photos, and Dr Danny Taglicht who clarified a few events in the story.

Chapter 1: Potsdam

Until 1918, when Germany became a democratic republic, the royal residences in the city of Potsdam, including the Sans Souci Palace (meaning 'without cares'), were the homes of the Prussian kings and the German Kaiser. After the 1st World War, Kaiser Wilhelm II abdicated, and was exiled to the Netherlands, but the palace remained the property of the Hohenzollern dynasty, and a landmark in the noble city of Potsdam.

A decade later, in 1928, Margarethe Stern was born to a middle class Jewish couple also living in Potsdam, situated some fifteen miles to the south-west of Berlin. Her parents, Jakob and Marlene, although proud to be Jewish, were not religious, and therefore did not observe the festivals, or actively practise Judaism. German, and not Yiddish, was spoken in the home, and it could be said that they were completely assimilated into the German way of life, to the point that Jakob had served his country as a doctor in the 1st World War. Before his marriage to Marlene in 1927, he had studied for several years, qualifying as an ophthalmologist and setting up his own clinic on Wilhelm Platz, with a spacious apartment attached. At this time, he was 46 years old, but his bride was only 22.

By 1930, Marlene had given birth to her second child, Susanne, completing the family, and the 2 children were sufficiently close to each other in age to play together, well provided for by their father whose work centred on a Jewish hospital in Berlin, as well as his own private Potsdam clinic. The two little girls led a happy life, since both parents were devoted to them, and they all enjoyed the liberating effect of employing servants in the apartment. Jakob had a widowed mother whom he supported, and 4 older sisters. His unmarried sister, Alma, came to live with the family, and the children loved her company. They also looked forward to Sunday visits from their maternal grandfather, a general practitioner, and sadly a widower, living in Berlin.

It should be said that following the 1st World War, the Treaty of Versailles imposed a huge debt on Germany that could be paid only in gold or foreign currency. When Germany failed to honour its reparation payments, France occupied the industrial Ruhr in order to enforce those payments. In losing all its gold, the German government tried to buy foreign currency with German currency. This caused the Deutsch Mark to fall in value, so the German government ordered the central bank to print more money which produced hyperinflation and disastrous results. The money became worthless, and people were literally forced to fill suitcases with banknotes in order to buy a loaf of bread.

After the Wall Street crash of 1929, the United States gave Germany 90 days to pay back all the money previously loaned to the country to support its faltering, post war economy. Industrial areas like the Ruhr went bankrupt, and millions of workers were laid off. Economically, the country was in dire straits, and prosperous Jews were able to invest their money abroad, provoking antisemitism on the part of millions of the unemployed who were unable to do so.

Fortunately for his family, Jakob did not find himself in a

vulnerable situation financially since his services as an eye doctor were both important and sought after, and additionally, he was able to provide employment for others. He was aware of the Nazi ideology of antisemitism as far back as 1920 in the 25 point Nazi Party Programme, and cognizant of what the consequences of the Nazis gaining power would be....at least as far as the Jews were concerned.

Disastrously, by 1931, exports had dropped, industrial production and agricultural prices fell, 5 major banks collapsed and 50,000 businesses went bankrupt; 6 million people became unemployed, many failing to feed their families or heat their homes. Economic hardships of the German people created in many of them a desire for change from the political status quo, in the hope of gaining a better life for themselves. Consequently, millions of Nazi voters did not cast their vote for the party because they were rabid anti-Semites; they accepted the Nazi Party's 1920 programme, including the anti-Semitic paragraph, if the party offered them food, jobs and hope for the future.

That said, Germany had a history of antisemitism, although that was by no means a German phenomenon. Apart from historically blaming Jews for the death of Christ (yet the Christian Creed states, 'suffered under Pontius Pilate'), in more recent times, the blame dated back to the Black Death in the 14th century for which the Jews were accused of causing, and this irrational hatred was more prevalent in some areas of the country than others. More recently still, the Jews were blamed for the country's defeat in World War 1 and the subsequent economic depression. Yet had Germany enjoyed a strong economy in those years, it is unlikely that the increase in antisemitism would have been so extreme, with less need to find a scapegoat. Too often human beings blame others when things go wrong, and envy played a part, as the Jews in Germany tended to be well-educated and prosperous.

During the 6 years of Hitler's dictatorship from 1933 until the outbreak of war in 1939, Jews were subjected to 400 decrees affecting their private and public lives; apart from the national laws against the Jews, additional ones, peculiar to each region, were also promulgated.

On 27th February 1933, Marinus Van Der Lubbe, a Dutch communist, was arrested for having set fire to the Reichstag building of the German Parliament, together with 4 other communists, and the Nazi party became convinced that communists generally were plotting against the German government. Their political antipathy was then directed towards 2 groups...Jews and Communists, and their plan was to dissolve parliament as quickly as possible to pave the way for dictatorship.

The Garrison Church in Potsdam, an 18th century Protestant baroque church, was until 1918, the parish church of the Prussian royal family. The kings of Prussia were buried there, including Frederick the Great, and Johann Sebastian Bach had played the organ there several times. Following the Reichstag fire some 3 weeks earlier, on 21st March, 1933, Adolf Hitler reconvened the new parliament, the Reichstag, in that church, and shook Reich President Hindenburg's hand. The opening ceremony on the 'Day of Potsdam' was a well-organised gathering to demonstrate unity between the Nazi Party and the old Prussian elite. Thus, Adolf Hitler and his supporters were legitimized, and the German Reich was born.

Chapter 2: Persecution

For the 523,000 Jews living in Germany in 1933, life soon deteriorated as soon as the Nazis seized power. No sooner had Hitler, as dictator, installed himself head of a National Socialist government, anti-Semitic laws were promulgated. Jews were removed from the Civil Service, and Jewish doctors were forbidden to work in charity hospitals. It is unlikely that Jakob would have lost his position at the Jewish hospital in Berlin at this point. That was to come later. What he would have noticed was the anti-Jewish atmosphere becoming more apparent as the months went by, and sporadic bouts of violence perpetrated on Jews by gangs of Aryan thugs, breaking into shops or private houses, and even committing murder.

Persecution progressed rapidly, particularly since an "Enabling Law" of March 1933 gave power to the Nazi Party to make laws without parliamentary approval. Thus radio, newspapers, leaflets and rallies were used to stir up anti-Semitic and anti-communist propaganda. In April of the same year, the Nazis led a nationwide boycott of Jewish businesses, and hundreds of Jews were rounded up by the Sturm Abteilung or SA(the Assault Division of storm troopers, dressed in their brown shirts) and sent to concentration camps, the earliest being Dachau, situated a few miles from Munich.

As time went on, Jewish lawyers were forbidden to practise, and closer to home as far as Jakob was concerned, Jewish doctors could no longer treat non-Jewish patients, and Jewish students were denied admission to medical schools. Jakob would, no doubt, have lost numerous patients following this edict.

When Shechita was banned, that is the Jewish method of slaughtering animals, the Stern family, as assimilated Germans, may have quickly adapted to a non-kosher way of choosing their food without too much of a problem, yet fully aware that their culture was under attack.

Margarethe was enrolled at a state primary school in Potsdam, despite a reduction of places made available for Jewish children, and Susanne joined her 2 years later. The text books were slanted with Nazi ideology and many teachers who were members of the Nazi party wore their uniforms in school. The children were required to salute several times a day with the accompanying words "Heil Hitler." In some schools, Jewish children were ordered to sit at the back of the class as if they were not really part of it; yet if the lesson centred on racial characteristics, so dear to Hitler's heart, they would be ordered to stand at the front of the class so that the pupils could study the difference in their physiognomies, the object of the lesson being to prove that Jews were an inferior race. This, in turn, encouraged bullying of the Jewish children by their non-Jewish classmates.

For non-Jewish Germans who were not left wing, life became tolerable. The French had left the Ruhr, and Hitler had managed to send millions of the unemployed back to work, roaring the industrial workplace into production. Consequently, many

Germans looked upon the Fuhrer as their saviour. In contrast, anti-Semitic Nazi policies were designed to bring about emigration on a large scale so that Germany would be free of Jews (Juden rein). And many prosperous Jews did leave early on, mostly to other European countries which would prove to be disastrous later. As the persecution of the Jews became more intense and comprehensive, the flow of emigrants increased, many to the United States, Great Britain, Palestine and Latin-America. Inevitably, many others were unwilling to uproot themselves or were unable to obtain visas or funds for emigration.

By 1935, Jews were no longer considered to be German citizens; they could not vote or hold public office, own rural property or marry Aryans. Since they were now considered aliens in the country of their birth, they were forced to pay double taxes. In 1936 Jewish doctors were barred from practising medicine in German institutions. Sachsenhausen concentration camp was opened, followed by Buchenwald in 1937. The situation was becoming desperate.

Events proved to be even more desperate in 1938 when all Jewish children were expelled from German state schools. By this time Margarethe was aged 10 years, and old enough to go out on her own during the day. She would wander around the streets of Potsdam relishing a sense of freedom, proud to be Jewish, and not particularly sad about being banned from school. She was unable to play in the parks with her friends, or visit the swimming pool and cinema, though. Those were banned to Jews, too. Jakob, who by now was closer to sixty than fifty, was disallowed from practising medicine and seriously wondering how and where to emigrate. He had never been a Zionist, and therefore Palestine was not of immediate appeal, nor did he know how he would be able to support the family if he could not practise as an ophthalmologist. With that in mind, he spent a few days at a 'Hachshara Farm' away from Potsdam to learn how to diversify his earning power, and that was how he came to miss Kristallnacht.

The Night of Broken Glass, as it translates, referring to the shards of shattered glass which littered the streets after Jewish-owned buildings, stores and synagogues had their windows smashed and their property looted or burned, was an organised pogrom against Jews all over Germany and Austria during the night of 9th to10th November 1938, perpetrated by SA paramilitary forces and German civilians. It presaged what was to come. The Nazis meant business, and from that date, any Jews who had previously soldiered on amid all the developing persecution over the previous five years, imagining and hoping that things would improve, on that November night they knew that the opposite was true. The Nazis were forcing emigration rather than encouraging it, and yet at the same time were imposing more and more onerous emigration taxes in their desire to reduce German Jewry to penury. Many of those who left were virtually poverty-stricken on arrival in their host countries.

From their apartment in Wilhelm-Platz, the following morning, Marlene, Margarethe and Susanne saw, in horror, smoke rising from the burning synagogue in their neighbourhood. On the pavement lay the shattered evidence of the attack on Jakob's clinic which Marlene was ordered to clear up. Her neighbour, whose husband had already been imprisoned for refusing to say 'Heil' (such a greeting was, he concluded, reserved only for addressing God) helped her dispose of the glass.

The result of Kristallnacht throughout Germany and Austria was the destruction of thousands of homes, shops and 586 synagogues. At least 91 Jews were murdered. Thousands more were rounded up and sent to concentration camps. To add insult to injury, all damage to Jewish businesses and dwellings had to be paid for by the Jewish business man or occupant, and insurance claims by Jews were confiscated in favour of the Reich. Many poor souls with no means to emigrate, desolated by what had happened, committed suicide.

After Kristallnacht, no Jew felt safe in Germany. Every day was lived in constant fear of arrest and imprisonment. From 1933, a constant stream of emigrants turned into a frantic flood of refugees in 1938/39, (fifty thousand in all), searching for countries to admit them. Most countries kept to their quotas, and once they were filled, refused to grant visas. By the outbreak of World War 2, about 70 thousand German and Austrian refugees, dating from 1933, had been admitted into Britain, plus approximately 10,000 Kindertransport children (whose parents, for the most part, were left to die in Europe).

All this emigration still only accounted for half the Jews in Germany. Tens of thousands were left behind, with nowhere to go. Jews, throughout the ages, became used to living with hardships, persecution and unfair treatment, and they may have thought that keeping a low profile was the best policy in the hope of better times to come, especially if they were close to being penniless. It was, perhaps, their only option, and they would never have imagined that persecution would turn to genocide.

Jakob and Marlene, however, were in no doubt at all that emigration was a necessity.

Chapter 3: Emigration

As with most parents who find themselves in a dangerous and volatile situation, the top priority in the lives of Jakob and Marlene was the welfare and protection of their children, so they were relieved to find a Jewish home cum small boarding school in Berlin where Margarethe and Susanne could stay in safety, and be well looked after, along with other Jewish children in a similar situation.

Sadly, the parents of many of those children had already been arrested and interned in concentration camps, causing, in consequence, a great deal of distress not only to themselves, but to the seemingly abandoned children. Tears and anxiety were a common occurrence, particularly at night.

It was in that home that the girls received not only love and care, but, for a short time a Jewish education with emphasis on the High Holy Days and festivals, especially Chanukah...which they loved, and which instilled in them a pride in their religion. Fortunately, they were not required to wear the Star of David badge on their outer clothing; that law would be introduced in 1941. Sometimes in the holidays, Margarethe and Susanne would stay either with their aunts, Jakob's sisters, two of whom were religious Jews who taught the girls about Judaism, or with close family friends.

Jakob and Marlene were then free to research the chances of emigration; a daunting task, with worryingly few possibilities. Most countries, having already received thousands of refugees, and unwilling or unable to accept tens of thousands more, closed their doors. In Palestine, riots continually breaking out between Arabs and Jews in the Mandate caused the British to apply stringent controls on immigration. Nevertheless, for Jakob it was still an option. America could provide visas for a doctor and family, but no earning power for 2 years owing to the United States' requirement of study and examinations for all doctors entering that country. Jakob needed to be employed as soon as possible, and was reluctant to accept charity.

Many thousands had applied to go to Central and South America, especially to Argentina, Chile, Brazil and Bolivia, but it was questionable as to whether there were definite job opportunities for Jakob in those countries. Later in 1939, several hundred refugees embarked on a passage to Cuba, but disastrously were unable to disembark at Havana, and were forced to return to Hamburg. Some of those refugees ended up in the gas chambers.

Kindertransport, a unique rescue operation commencing shortly after Kristallnacht, offered refuge in Great Britain to approximately 10,000 Jewish children from Germany, Austria and Czechoslovakia. Jewish and non-Jewish agencies, especially the Quakers, offered to fund the operation, and every child would have a guarantee of 50 pounds sterling to finance his or her eventual re-emigration. Jakob was interested, made contact with the Kindertransport office in Berlin of World Jewish Relief, and completed the necessary forms, learning that his daughters would be placed in 2 separate homes, and not together. No doubt it was the fact that Margarethe and Susanne would be split up, and that he might never see them again, caused him to change his mind and withdraw their names from the departure list, much to the official's chagrin.

Marlene and Jakob, therefore, needed to find a plan of escape from the German Reich for the whole family, and word was passed through influential Jewish contacts that the one place where they would be admitted without visas was China. It has to be remembered that they were stateless, since their German nationality had been withdrawn years before. It so happened that the authorities of both Shanghai and Harbin in Manchuria (known then as Manchukuo) were accepting Jewish doctors in an attempt to rescue them and their expertise from Nazi-dominated Germany, Austria and Czechoslovakia. Jakob was invited to work in the Jewish hospital in Harbin, so in order to keep his family safe and together, he would have to move them half way round the world.

Who were the authorities of Harbin, Manchuria, in north-eastern China? They were not Chinese, since Japan had invaded that part of the country in 1931, and then Shanghai in 1937. The Jews had an interesting history in Harbin since the Russo-Manchurian Treaty of 1897 granted the Russians the concession of building the Chinese Eastern Railway which opened in1903. Harbin became the administrative capital, and Russian Jewish families moved there, not to work on the railway but to develop commerce as shopkeepers, contractors, bankers and restauranteurs. And so out of a desolate area comprising only a few cottages and a bitterly cold winter climate, a thriving city was borne, with shops, schools, synagogues (churches and a cathedral for the non-Jewish population later on) and a Jewish hospital.

One of the great attractions of Harbin for the Russian Jews during the reign of Tsar Nicolas 11 was to be removed from state-controlled antisemitism, and to live their lives in peace and equality. From 1917 onwards, more Russians arrived, White Russians this time, fleeing the Russian Revolution and Civil War, and bringing their anti-Semitic prejudice with them, though at least it was not organised by the state. The population grew, and the languages spoken in the city were Russian, Chinese, a little German, English, and after 1931, Japanese. By1933/34 a number of eminent Jewish doctors from Germany had been invited to Harbin by the Japanese which coincided with their suppression under the Nazis, and their desire to leave that country.

The Japanese respected the Jews, their wealth, power, and above all their ability to influence world events. They remembered, and were impressed that Jewish finance had enabled Japan to purchase sufficient armaments to win the Russo-Japanese war of 1905. How and why did this happen? Extremely wealthy Jews, both in America and world-wide, were so incensed by the Tsar's ruthless persecution of the Jews in Russia over a long period that they made sure the Russians were defeated.

Another reason for the Japanese to respect the Jews was a book written in Russia in 1903 entitled 'The

Protocols of the Elders of Zion', and, as a complete forgery, was the work of the Russian Secret Police...the Okhrana. The forgery, the most anti-Semitic document in history, circulated far and wide, including to Japan. The protocols refer to the minutes of a meeting of world Jewish leaders which supposedly took place every 100 years for the purpose of plotting how to manipulate and control the world in the next century.

The Japanese were allegedly taken in by this document, and seemingly respected the Jews even more, in the hope that they could influence history in their favour yet again. Thus, their treatment of the Jews in Harbin was even-handed, fair and free from state antisemitism which was good news for Jakob, Marlene, Margarethe and Susanne.

And what became of Jakob's sisters in the theatre of war? His eldest sister, Adele, managed to take her family to the United States, but the other three sisters...Rosa, Betty, and also Alma, the children's favourite aunt, decided to remain in Germany, and did not survive. As for Marlene's 3 siblings, her sister Lotte died tragically at a young age, but not in the concentration camps, Heinz emigrated to England, and Fritz, having spent time in Buchenwald, was released with the help of his brother, and headed for Shanghai to spend the war years in the Jewish Hongkew ghetto there. Close friends of the Stern family stayed in Germany and died in Theresienstadt where about 100,000 souls perished, not in the gas chambers, but from starvation and disease. Survival very much depended on making the decision to escape at the right time, which was not possible for everyone.

Chapter 4: Escape!

The Stern children stayed with relatives and friends whilst their parents set about solving the considerable problem of organising their departure for the Far East as quickly as possible. Each month more and more anti-Semitic laws were introduced to increase the misery of the Jews. Unsurprisingly, the suicide rate had greatly increased. At this date, Shanghai was the last resort for escape...12 thousand refugees arrived in 1939 alone...and thousands more without a sea passage, desperate to escape Hitler's clutches at all costs, crossed Russia, the Urals and Siberia by the Trans - Siberian Railway to reach Shanghai by land. The numbers reached 20,000, some needing financial assistance. The Soviet Union terminated this escape route later in 1939.

Tens of thousands of Jewish men had been arrested for virtually no reason at all, and sent to concentration camps from which they were unable to secure a release unless they could provide valid travel papers. Marlene's brother, Heinz, who had emigrated to England with his father, was able to extricate their brother Fritz from Buchenwald by providing him with travel papers for Shanghai. Without that kind of support, there was little chance of survival in the future.

As with all Jewish emigrants from Germany and Austria who owned property, Jakob could not sell his apartment and clinic so as to take the money with him or invest it abroad. He was forced to leave his financial assets in the profiteering hands of the Nazis with no reimbursement whatsoever. He had no rights, and no amount of arguing out the ethics of the case with the authorities would have improved the situation. On the contrary, it would probably have landed him in Dachau. Better and safer to say nothing, to make plans and accept the insulting 10 Reichs Marks of currency per head on leaving the country. Jewellery had to be handed in, although many escapees tried to hide it on their person by sewing it into their clothing, but with customary teutonic thoroughness, Nazi checks for anything of value were organised on trains leaving Germany. Marlene entrusted her jewellery for safe keeping to friends who were leaving for Holland, but she never saw it again. All Jewish property and assets reverted to the German government.

Within an increasingly depressing situation, one advantage which the Nazis had overlooked was furniture and household possessions. It was still possible to organise a lift (a very large crate) so that heavy items, which in the Sterns' case included the contents of Jakob's clinic, could be transported by sea to China. At first it seemed that the Nazi authorities were merely interested in illegally gaining property and businesses, finance, liquid cash, jewellery and works of art, but as time went on, their greed increased and, yet again, new laws were introduced. The Sterns were one of the last families to benefit from this liberal oversight.

In 1936, the liner Conte Biancamano, amongst others, was chartered by the company Lloyd Triestino for voyages to the Far East, mostly involving the transport of thousands of Jews fleeing Nazi Germany to Shanghai with no visa requirements. It was a beautiful liner, built in the William Beardmore shipyard at Dalmuir in Scotland in 1925, but had been recently refurbished to a luxurious specification, with an open air swimming pool, a white hull and yellow funnels. In January 1939, with just one suitcase each, the Stern family left friends, relatives and Germany forever to travel by train through the Alps to Italy where the liner was docked at Genoa. Jakob had tried to persuade Alma to accompany them, but she made the disastrous decision to stay in Germany with her sisters. Before Jakob and family embarked, and prepared for their 3 week voyage, 2 German non-Jewish ladies who had travelled with them to see them off presented them with a typewriter; an apt and touching valedictory gift which was to prove very useful in the years to come.

Thoughts on leaving Europe, perhaps unspoken to the children, would have filled the minds of Jakob and Marlene with passionate and bitter resentment. How could this unmitigated disaster happen to the Jews after generations of loyal service to Germany? They had really loved the country...its achievements, culture, music and literature, and they, too, had contributed to its greatness. Unlike the Jews of Poland with their inward-looking Hassidic traditions, German Jews had been totally assimilated into the German way of life, and were proud to be German, dispensing with Yiddish, and even with their religion in some cases...Felix Mendelssohn, Heinrich Heine, Eduard Bendemann, Fritz Haber and Gustave Mahler as known examples. Then the movement for Reform Judaism, started in Germany, adopted more of the vernacular and less

Hebrew, so that the result was Germanised. In many cases, Jewish citizens thought themselves as German first and Jewish second. And what more could one do to express loyalty to one's country than serve it in time of war? Life had never been just or easy for the Jews en masse, but this was preposterous and vile beyond belief. And was not that great work of Beethoven, the 9th Symphony, about the brotherhood of man, reason and social justice for all?

Life on the Conte Biancamano was the antithesis of everything they had experienced under Nazi suppression in the previous 6 years, and like their fellow refugees, the Stern family enjoyed the luxury of their surroundings; the delicious food in abundance with considerate stewards in attendance, entertainment and on deck activities. Most important of all, was the freedom from fear and antisemitism, violence and hatred...and being together as a family. Constant worry and stress were replaced by relaxation and relief, at least temporarily, which was appreciated more by their parents than by Margarethe and her sister.

Crossing the Mediterranean towards Egypt was an emotional experience; on the way, glimpsing the coast of Palestine as a family...the Promised Land, the land of their forefathers, so near and yet unobtainable...and then down the Suez Canal to the Red Sea; from the January cold of Germany to the warmer climes of the Middle East.

Port Said was the first stopping port and city, lying to the north-east of Egypt, and established in 1859 during the building of the Suez Canal. It had become an important port for Egyptian exports and a fuelling station for ships that would pass through the Suez Canal. Passengers did not disembark until the liner had progressed through the Red Sea, and reached Aden, a port city in Yemen administered by the British between 1839 and 1967. It is situated on the eastern approach to the Red Sea and its natural harbour lies in the crater of a dormant volcano.

There they were all in for a shock. Having no money except for the 10 Marks each which could not be spent unwisely, the Sterns, amongst others, were unable to buy souvenirs from the waiting vendors who became infuriated with their lack of sales, and shouted at them in frustrated rage. It was also the first time that the girls had seen native Africans, and were both fascinated and fearful of them. Resident Jews in Aden showed them around the port, but were equally disappointed that the refugees could afford to buy nothing from them, as they were no doubt dependent on the generous custom of supposedly prosperous passengers from luxurious liners. Shockingly memorable in the intense desert heat was the terrible sight of poor lepers, distinctive by their facial nodules, lesions and deformities, begging for money on every street corner...something never encountered in Europe. Returning to the ship proved to be something of a relief, despite their nurturing a sense of compassion for those victims of a terrible disease.

This experience may well have influenced their attitude to seeing the sights at the future ports on their itinerary...Bombay, Singapore, Manila, Hong Kong and finally Shanghai; over 9 thousand miles from Genoa. Fear of potential violence, disease and the unexpected would have been uppermost in the minds of Jakob and Marlene, but for Margarethe and Susanne, the experience was an adventure not to be missed.

It was a case of enjoying the voyage across the vast Indian Ocean to the Far East as an end in itself, but Marlene and Jakob harboured worries about the safety and welfare of their relatives and friends left behind in Germany to face unknown developments of that devilish persecution, about how life would be for themselves in Shanghai, and not least about the imminence of war. In fact, when the Conte Biancamano reached Hong Kong, and they all heard sporadic shooting, Jakob was convinced that war had already broken out, but it was simply the firework celebrations for the Chinese New Year!

Jakob Stern in the late 1930s

Margarethe Stern, aged 8 or 9

Margarethe aged 10 or 11

Margarethe and Susanne with their aunt Alma c. 1938

Margarethe and Susanne at the sea-side c 1933/34

Marlene Stern, mother of Margarethe and Susanne

Jakob Stern before WW2

Jakob Stern with Margarethe and Susanne on a picnic in Germany.

Chapter 5: Shanghai

Situated on China's east coast, the city of Shanghai is actually centred on the Huang Pu River, a tributary of the great Yangtse River which flows out into the East China Sea and beyond into the Pacific. Most of its land is flat, lying on the alluvial plain, and, as one of the biggest ports in the world, provides easy access into the interior of China. It experiences a humid, subtropical climate with typhoons, occasional downpours and freak thunderstorms.

It has an interesting history. Following the Opium Wars and the Treaty of Nanking in 1842, the British forced China to open 5 ports, including Shanghai, for trade with the West; the other ports were Canton, Ningpo, Fuchow and Amoy, and the Island of Hong Kong was ceded to the United Kingdom until 1997. The British, rightly or wrongly, did not accept China's isolationist policy; they wished to buy porcelain, silks and tea, and to develop Chinese trade with the West. Therefore, from 1845 onwards, foreigners in Shanghai lived in 3 settlements...the British, the American and the French. By 1863, the British and Americans had joined together, forming the International Settlement, but the French concession remained separate.

Much later in 1937, following the Battle of Shanghai, the city was occupied by the Japanese, and the port allowed entry to those without visa or passport. By the time the Ashkenazi Jews arrived in the late 1930s, fleeing Nazi Germany, 2 other Jewish communities had long since settled in the city; the wealthy

Sephardic Baghdadi Jews, including the Sassoon, Hardoon and Kadoorie families in the mid 19th century, and also the Russian Jews who had fled from the anti-Semitic pogroms of Tsarist Russia, forming the Russian community of Shanghai, in addition to that of Harbin, Manchuria.

The immigration of Ashkenazi Jews from Germany, Austria, and Poland continued until December 1941, when the Japanese attacked Pearl Harbour. Almost immediately Japanese soldiers stormed into the International Settlement. The extraterritorial privileges enjoyed by the British and Americans for 100 years ceased to exist. Many were arrested, tortured, starved, beaten and hauled off to numerous labour camps run by the Imperial Japanese Army. This cruel treatment was not perpetrated on the recently arrived Jews from Germany, Austria and Poland, but their living conditions and general standard of living worsened as the war continued.

The religious centre for the Russian Jewish community since 1907 was around the Ohel Moshe Synagogue in the Hongkew (now Hongkou) district of Shanghai, and it was in that area from 1943 onwards that the Japanese consolidated the housing of thousands of European Jews, regarding them as stateless persons, into a ghetto of barely a square mile. About 100,000 Chinese continued to live alongside them in that crowded area, and, if anything, were poorer than the Jewish refugees. The ghetto area was not walled or surrounded by barbed wire, but passes were required for entering or leaving; it was patrolled, and a curfew was enforced. Disappearing Caucasians would have easily been spotted by the Japanese.

When in 1939 the penniless German-speaking refugees arrived in Shanghai, they were received by a committee aboard ship, but then walked ashore without showing their passports or papers. Members of the Jewish community were waiting and looking for relatives they expected. Then the refugees were directed onto trucks and moved to a reception area where they were housed and given food. Most of them were accommodated in the poor Hongkew district of Shanghai, because they could not afford anything better. Finding work proved very difficult, they had been stripped of their assets by the Nazis, and consequently many refugees had to accept charity. The well-established Sephardic Jews provided some financial assistance, as did the Joint Distribution Committee in New York, organising shelters converted from former barracks, with 10 to a room, hard, narrow beds, food distributed in soup kitchens amid near starvation. It was worlds away from the luxury of the liner they had just left behind.

Disease through poor hygiene was a major problem. Scarlet fever killed over100 people in shelters during 1939, and by the end of 1944, hunger and infection had killed about 1,000 Jewish refugees.

In China, for centuries, human excrement, known as night soil, was used to fertilize the land which helped it to retain crucial nutrients and perennial fertility, but the practice also caused problems for public health. Pathogens could be transferred to both humans and food because the bacteria was attached to the produce in the soil. Therefore, eating raw vegetation was extremely dangerous. Cooking vegetables was important, and disease could be prevented by soaking fruit in chemicals before eating. Another problem was personal hygiene, or lack of it. Dormitories were filled to over capacity, and one washroom was shared by everyone; hot water could only be bought in stores, so bathing was a problem. Disease was rampant. Other problems included a sense of isolation from the rest of their known world, their worry about relatives and friends left behind in Europe, their struggle with the Chinese, Japanese and Russian languages, and their continuing poverty.

Despite these formidable problems, many refugees started to adapt to life in Shanghai. They opened schools for their children, developed a social life around the synagogue, initiated newspapers, started up small cafés, Kosher butchers, German delicatessens, theatres, sports clubs and even cabarets. Jewish cultural life became alive and vibrant.

In July 1942, the Nazis made every effort to exterminate the Jews of Shanghai now that their official allies were the Japanese. Meisinger, previously known as 'the butcher of Warsaw', had become the Japan-based Gestapo Chief Delegate and was ordered to implement the 'Shanghai Final Solution Scheme.' To their credit, the Japanese did not agree to slaughtering the Jews, nor did they hand them over to the Nazis. Instead they placed all the Jews together in the Hongkew ghetto where overall control of them could be maintained and where they suffered from war shortages, but no violence or ill-treatment from the

Japanese. Nor did they receive any anti-Semitism or ill-treatment from the Chinese who lived alongside them; in fact, on 17th July, 1945, when American aircraft accidentally bombed the Hongkew ghetto, the Jews and the Chinese combined efforts to transport the wounded to the clinics and hospitals and to care for them, regardless of their ethnic origin.

Jewish refugees were only able to leave Shanghai when the Japanese surrendered, the city being officially liberated on 3rd September, 1945, but they had survived the war, thanks to both the Japanese and the Chinese, and above all to the Jewish charities. Many emigrated to the USA via Taiwan, to Canada, Australia, South America, and others back to Europe. When the State of Israel was declared in 1948, many of the Shanghai refugees emigrated there as soon as possible, but they did not forget Shanghai.

The Stern family, as passengers of the Conte Biancamano, would have had time enough to survey the city from the ship as it lay at anchor in the estuary of the Yangtze, and what they saw would have horrified them. Slums and ruined buildings, piles of rubble and refuse, wharves and warehouses lined the shore, and beyond the water's edge, more and more slums. Little did the other refugees know at that point that those slums would be their own homes for the next 5 or 6 years. Approaching the jetty, a mixture of odours assaulted them...of dirt and decay, of street cooking and disease, of excrement and poverty, of sweat and opium. Had there been any other safer destinations in fleeing from the Nazis in 1939, Jakob, and many like him with children, would have chosen a more wholesome alternative. After all, Shanghai was one of the most crime-ridden and prostitute-ridden cities in the world, full of thieves, pickpockets and beggars where life was cheap. But there was no choice, and they simply had to make the best of it.

Jakob and Marlene found a hotel, and after the children had had supper, they undressed and settled down to sleep while their parents met up with other fellow refugees in a nearby restaurant. Before long, the little girls, dressed in their outer clothes and looking scared, confronted their parents with the story that a strange Chinaman had entered their bedroom, and used the bathroom. There was no harm done, but their parents took them back to the hotel and did not leave them again. It was the first lesson of acclimatising themselves to life in Shanghai.

The next day Marlene was delighted and relieved to be reunited with her brother, Fritz, who had already completed his voyage to Shanghai, and was settled in Hongkew where the Japanese had been very much in evidence since 1937.The whole family was glad to see him and could witness for themselves the poverty, primitive conditions and total lack of privacy there, and could develop a learning curve of what not to do in order to remain alive. For example, on no account drink the water (unless boiled) or clean teeth with the water or drink milk, consume raw vegetables and fruit, as typhoid fever and death would be the likely outcome. It was advisable not to enter the Old Chinese City or the Japanese area of Hongkew, and not to carry valuables on their person and not to trust policemen. Malaria might result from a mosquito bite, and typhus could develop from a flea bite. In such poor, dirty surroundings and a subtropical climate, the likelihood of developing any of these diseases was quite high. For all that, Fritz remained in Hongkew throughout the war, survived, and then was able to emigrate to the United States.

The sight of penniless yet well-dressed European refugees leaving the ship, their luggage carried by poverty-stricken coolies in rags was bizarre, as was the frenetic roar of the traffic, the rickshaws drawn by Chinamen on foot crying out their rates, the carts and wheelbarrows. It bore no resemblance to the gentle elegance of the traditional Chinese pictures of the Willow Patterns. It was a much harder world, a world in which whole families lived on small boats, cooking, washing their laundry in the filthy water, and where children were born and died of infection, their little bodies wrapped in a bamboo mat and left to float in the river. The stench was unrelenting and powerful.

It was also a world of scarlet fever and tuberculosis where, thanks to the Joint Distribution Committee of New York, there were soup kitchens for the hungry refugees, a daily loaf of bread and money for the destitute. All, regardless of their individual situations, were deeply grateful that they had found sanctuary in Shanghai.

As for Jakob, his decision was always to travel to Harbin in Manchuria where he was to join the medical community in that city, so in spite of being invited by the Jewish community in Shanghai to stay and work in their Jewish hospital, he declined. From all that he and

Marlene had observed in a short time, they concluded that Shanghai, from several points of view, was not a healthy environment in which to raise children.

Chapter 6: Dalniy, Dairen, Dalian.

In order to make their way to Manchuria, or Manchukuo as the Japanese called it, the Stern family needed to take another ship and travel across the Yellow Sea to Dairen, and they did not delay.

Again the history is both interesting and revealing. In the 19th century, China had lost out in wars at various times to the British, the Russians and the Japanese, and as a consequence, much of her territory was leased for commercial purposes by those victorious foreign powers. In 1898, after gaining control of the Kwantang Leased Territory of South Manchuria, the Russians built a modern commercial port city which was ice-free and which became linked to the Trans-Siberian Railway from Harbin; they called the city Dalniy, meaning 'remote' or 'distant', and the port, Port Arthur, a naval base, some 27 miles to the east, served western traders.

Following the victory of the Japanese in the Russo-Japanese war of 1905, its name changed to Dairen, and the Empire of Japan occupied the region until 1945. It became the main trading port between Manchuria and Japan, and massive Japanese investment was concentrated in that city. The South Manchurian Railway was headquartered there, and some of its profits transformed Dairen into a modern city with modern architecture, hospitals, universities and a large industrial area. Later still in 1950, when the city had been returned to the Chinese, the name changed again to Dalian...

which remains today.

Therefore, when Jakob and family arrived, the city was under Japanese control and called Dairen, yet architecturally and to some extent in its town planning, it was Russian, with its iconic buildings, beautiful shops and wide streets, lined with trees and flowers. All newcomers, including the Sterns, were impressed with its fresh sea air, seashore, parks, hills and pleasant walks around the city...far more health-giving, and safer than Shanghai. In fact, many visiting Russians spent their holidays there.

The Russian Jewish residents who welcomed the Sterns were both kind and hospitable, accommodating the family temporarily in the house of friends. But linguistic problems immediately arose, since the Russians were amazed that a Jewish family could speak no Yiddish, and certainly no Russian! Fortunately, they all shared some command of English, yet the main languages of Dairen were Russian, Japanese and Chinese which presented a challenge to the incoming German refugees, who tended to cling together socially. In addition to the Russian Jews, white Russians having fled the revolution, and some quite prosperous, had also settled in the city, yet despite the proximity of so many Russians, the family did not make a determined effort to learn Russian whilst in Dairen, perhaps uncertain of what the language situation would be in their final destination, Harbin.

Apart from problems with communication, Jakob was anxious to earn money and not be dependent on charity whilst waiting to complete the journey to Harbin in North

Manchuria (Manchukuo) where he would be employed as an ophthalmologist. Although Harbin, again, had been controlled by the Japanese since 1931, it was independent, and therefore visas were required for entry, so the family had to stay in Dairen whilst waiting for them to be granted. It was there that Margarethe celebrated her 11th birthday, whilst they were staying at the hotel Eldorado, by the sea, and received a large and memorable pencil sharpener as a present, reminding her that many months had passed since she and Susanne had been expelled from their school in Potsdam.

The major problem in Dairen concerned their luggage which had been transported from Germany by ship in a lift of large crates, including furniture, pictures, a library, kitchen appliances and Jakob's whole ophthalmic clinic. After travelling for thousands of miles, the ship had disastrously run aground between Shanghai and Dairen, and when Jakob discussed the problem of retrieving their belongings from the stricken ship whilst he was at the German Embassy, he was shouted at, and informed in glacial terms by the Nazi officials there that he would have to pay for the damage himself. Hardly possible for someone who had left Germany with only 10 Reich Marks to his name. Thoroughly dispirited, Jakob returned to the family, wondering how he was to pay this bill, and whether they would lose all their possessions. That evening, another official from the Embassy called to see Jakob,and clearly ashamed to witness how rudely and cruelly he had been treated that morning, offered to lend him the money needed to save the lift from the wrecked ship. Jakob thanked him but refused the offer. Fortunately, the Jewish community loaned him the money to release the belongings which they were finally reunited with in Harbin some weeks later.

After spending almost three months in Dairen, the Sterns, glad to receive the long-expected visas granting them access to Harbin, were invited to a Russian Jewish brunch. Unused to Russian etiquette, and thrust into a quick, culinary learning curve, they chose several hors d'oeuvres thinking them to be entrées and therefore the entire meal, only to be faced later with the fish, then the soup, the meat and finally the dessert! That was Russian custom. They also learned that in Russia it is polite to leave a little on one's plate to indicate that one has eaten enough, whereas in Germany it was considered impolite to leave anything at all on one's plate.

Dairen was a pleasant city, the family had been well-treated there, and friendships had been made which would last not only during their stay in China, but in the years to come. However, their journey had been long and they were yet to reach their destination. They were all anxious to settle down into their new life in Harbin where Jakob would confront the challenge of practising his profession in a new country, and would earn money, without the worry and indignity of accepting charity, where Marlene would create a loving and comfortable home for them all, where the whole family would experience very real linguistic problems, and where the children would have to knuckle down to revitalising their education after more than six months with no schooling.

Chapter 7: Harbin

The number of Russian Jews entering Harbin increased after World War I and the Bolshevik Revolution, so that by the 1920s, the figure reached about 20,000. It became something of a boom town. Jews enjoyed equality with non-Jews, and were given complete freedom of religion, cultural and educational autonomy. They became furriers, shop keepers, restauranteurs, entrepreneurs, hoteliers, teachers, artists and doctors, starting their own National Bank in 1923, developing a prosperous, dynamic life and establishing a library, a Talmud Torah (a Jewish primary school, teaching Hebrew and the Scriptures), 2 synagogues, numerous Jewish-owned shops, a soup kitchen, a home for the aged, a Jewish hospital which treated both Jewish and non-Jewish patients, and also the Harbin Jewish Cemetery.

Fortunately for them, Russian became the lingua franca for both Jews and non-Jews alike in the city, including the Chinese, and better still, the Chinese had no history of antisemitism. This good fortune was not to last. When Harbin came under Japanese occupation in 1931, ugly events developed. Thousands of non-Jewish anti-Bolshevik White Russians who had also settled in Harbin, had brought antisemitism with them and established the Harbin Russian Fascist Party, which although was not organised by the State, involved itself in double dealing, extortion and the bullying of Jews by Russian gangsters. These crimes were permitted by the Japanese Army who expropriated private property and terrorised the civilian population.

This virulent antisemitism culminated in 1933 in the kidnap and murder of Simeon Caspé, the pianist son of a wealthy Harbin Jew who owned several properties, including the Hotel Moderne, and who refused to pay the ransom. The young man was tortured, his ears cut off and he was finally killed. Following this ghastly incident, the Japanese conducted a half-hearted approach to solving the crime, clearly wanting to curry favour with the numerous, influential White Russians in the city. Many Jews, then, chose to leave Harbin, and headed for cities like Shanghai and Tientsin which had not been invaded by the Japanese as yet. After the outbreak of Sino-Japanese hostilities in 1937, the Jewish population declined yet again, and before World War 2, many had departed for Australia and Brazil, or had made aliyah to Israel... which then was the Palestinian Mandate.

By the time Jakob and family reached Harbin at the beginning of September 1939, the Jewish population had been reduced to about 5,000. On arriving in the city, the family stayed in a hotel on the main street. It was none other than the Hotel Moderne itself, which boasted a restaurant, a cinema, a billiard room, a bar and a barber shop. Out of the three languages spoken in Harbin, Japanese, Chinese and Russian, the family decided to put their efforts into learning Russian, since that was the language spoken by the Jews, and much used elsewhere. They would have noticed the elegant, western-styled buildings, to them looking surprisingly European and new, many of which had been built by Jews, interspersed with those of a more Asian style, and they would have admired the theatres, cinemas, schools and beautiful shops.

A few days after their arrival and whilst on the balcony of their hotel room, Margarethe learned one of her first pieces of Russian vocabulary, shouted out by a paper boy in the street below..'. Voina' meaning 'war'. What they had been dreading had become reality, and their thoughts immediately turned to relatives and friends left behind in Germany. Marlene's brothers and father had found sanctuary, but Jakob's three sisters had not. Rosa and Betty were married and had stayed with their husbands, but Alma was single, and Jakob tortured himself for not having successfully persuaded her to board the Conte Biancamano with Marlene and the girls. Many other refugees must have felt similarly about leaving their relatives, and the guilt never left them.

Their stay at the Hotel Moderne quickly came to an end, and they moved into a rented flat. It was neither comfortable nor clean, but rather plagued with bedbugs, so Marlene set about rectifying those problems with washing, cleaning and disinfectant to make life more tolerable. Each morning a woman would arrive with the day's shopping, and teach the children a bit of Russian by using vegetables as visual aids. 'This is a carrot,' or 'This is a potato,' she would repeat, exercising her deep voice with some gravitas, which Margarethe and Susanne did not take at all seriously, and laughed behind her back, as mischievous children would.

Soon their next move to a very pleasant house with a small, enclosed garden was a joy and relief to them all, especially as their belongings miraculously arrived from the wrecked ship, and they were able to enjoy the comfort of their own home again...their own beds, furniture, the pictures, the wonderful library, and most important of all, the equipment for Jakob's clinic. The house came with a Chinese cook, and had belonged to a Jewish family who had left China for the United States, and it was there that the Sterns stayed until the day they left Harbin. After having taken painful leave of Germany and being en route for many months, they felt truly happy and grateful for their good fortune.

Having established a home, the next priority concerned Jakob's work, and it was not long before he was employed as an ophthalmologist at the Jewish Hospital in Harbin, and then was able to make preparations to open his own private clinic. His hopes and plans were coming to fruition. Soon his clinic was always full, and many of the patients arrived not only from Harbin and district, but from as far away as Mongolia. This was because Jakob could provide them with treatment for trachoma, (well before the existence of antibiotics) which is an infection of the eyes, can result in blindness after repeated infections, and occurs where people live in overcrowded conditions with limited access to water. As expected, language was a problem when communicating with the patients, so Jakob managed to gain the help of a Russian woman who translated for the Russian patients, and the cook translated for the Chinese patients.

Each evening, after surgery, all the windows were opened for a long time so that the waiting room could recover from an overwhelming smell of garlic permeating everything. So many of the Chinese people were short of money that Jakob would treat some of them at home, free of charge, whilst others paid not only with money, but also in kind, with presents of all sorts. Treatment at the Jewish Hospital cost 5 yens for all patients, Jew and non-Jew alike. Jakob's reputation as a successful eye-doctor became well-known in the area.

The children's education presented Marlene with something of a challenge. Both Margarethe and Susanne were enrolled at the Jewish Primary School, the Talmud Torah, where the studies were mostly in Russian, plus some Hebrew, and owing to their age difference, Susanne was placed in the first class and Margarethe in the second. The studies in the second class were complicated by the addition of Japanese to the curriculum (reflecting the Japanese occupation), which Margarethe did not appreciate one bit, but no doubt both children were absorbing Russian more quickly and easily than their parents. Fortunately for Susanne, a private school was found for her age group where the studies were in English, but the teachers were Russian. Margarethe was less fortunate since she had to stay at the Talmud Torah until the curriculum at the private school could accommodate her age group which took quite some time, and where she stayed for about two years.

The deteriorating relationship between the Soviets and the Japanese after the Battle of Khalkhin Gol which took place in 1939 on the Mongolian-Manchurian border and which the Soviets won decisively, may have prevented the Japanese from further aggression during the war. Within Harbin, however, where the Japanese were very much in control, they were able to close down the private school attended by Margarethe and Susanne, probably on the grounds that the headteacher was a Soviet Russian citizen.

The family had to accustom themselves to long and bitterly cold winters, the coldest of all amongst the Chinese cities, and short, cool summers with considerable rainfall. In the spring, gritty dust from Mongolia turned the skies yellow and covered every surface. Despite this, the Sterns, both adults and children, adapted well to their life in Harbin and interacted positively with the other German and Austrian immigrants, enjoying a lively, social life together. All the families were thriving and prospering, and the children's command of Russian had developed so well that they were able to communicate with local children as well as the immigrant children.

Summer, particularly, brought joyful opportunities of hiring a dacha, or house for the summer, where Jakob, Marlene, Margarethe and Susanne could stay with other families, enjoy holidays together and relax. On those occasions, Jakob would row a boat across the River Sungari, the family would swim and go fishing together, their enjoyment inspiring memories to be treasured in the future.

Chapter 8: Changes

By 1943, the Stern family had been comfortably settled in Harbin for three and a half years, and Jakob, at 63 years of age and in good health, had become eminent in his capacity as an ophthalmologist to both the Russian and the Chinese communities in the city, and well beyond. It could be said that in a relatively short time, he had really made a name for himself. Consequently, from time to time, he enjoyed a social life with friends, resulting from his professional success. In March 1943, he was invited to a dinner party, and shortly after that occasion, he fell terribly ill with typhoid fever, and tragically died on 31st March.

According to Jewish law, the body must be interred as soon as possible after death. Therefore, the funeral planning begins immediately, and the body must not be left alone until the time of burial. For these reasons, Jakob was buried the next day in the Harbin Jewish Cemetery. Many people attended the funeral...patients, friends and colleagues...to pay their respects, and to support Marlene, Margarethe and Susanne in their shocked and raw bereavement.

Marlene and her daughters realised that Jakob's death had resulted from insufficient care taken for the dinner party in the preparation of uncooked vegetables or fruit, and that the food or water he had consumed was contaminated. It was both sad and ironic that after suffering years of antisemitism in Germany, and after exerting a brave and noble effort to protect his family by travelling half way round the world to avoid death, he should lose his life from food poisoning. Marlene, Susanne and Margarethe were numb and bewildered with grief, very aware of being alone in a foreign country, without relatives or means of financial support.

Throughout the following week, Jakob's Chinese patients who had not already received news of his death, arrived at his clinic and did not want to believe that their doctor had died. Some of them even opened the clinic door to make quite sure, such was their respect and admiration for Jakob.

Apart from their loss of a husband and father, Jakob's tragic and unexpected death brought many changes to the Sterns' way of life, and their need to earn a living of some sort. Shortly after the funeral, Marlene advised the Chinese cook to look for another position since she would be unable to pay him a decent salary, and was prepared to take on the cooking duties herself. Touchingly, the cook refused to leave on the grounds that he had occupied the house before the Sterns, and had grown fond of them. It was true that he checked on their welfare in many caring ways, especially advising the children what to wear in Harbin's wintry weather. His devotion to the family was certainly reciprocated, and he became an indispensable member of the household until he passed away a few years later, working right up till a short time before his death.

Marlene's other economies involved selling the contents of Jakob's clinic, and she received advice from friends on how best to invest the money. Then she let out 2 rooms. The larger one, that of the clinic, was rented to a ballerina and her husband, and the smaller one to a single woman. However, that income was still insufficient for the family to maintain an acceptable standard of living, so at the end of the academic year, Margarethe, having reached her 15th birthday, decided to leave school to pursue a course in dressmaking, quickly learning how to use the sewing machine at home so as to provide herself with some earning power. Susanne was then only 13 years old, and therefore still of school age.

With great resolve, Margarethe successfully completed the course, and later became an apprentice seamstress to a fashionable salon in the city where fortunately the owner was Jewish. She was less fortunate in that she was the only Jewish seamstress and surrounded by an anti-Semitic and superstitious work force, but she was determined to persevere, to get on with them all, and to be a success.

Money was tight, and Margarethe's salary was definitely needed at home, although she was still very young to take on such responsibilities. The devoted Chinese cook recognised her as the family breadwinner, and always served her first at dinner. As the months passed, she managed to earn enough money to become an independent dressmaker, additionally making clothes for herself, her mother and sister. Life continued in this way for the Stern family until the summer of 1945 when more changes would come their way.

War in Europe had come to an end, and the tragic and detailed information of what later became known as the Holocaust was filtering through to all parts of the world. Hostilities, still continuing in the Far East with tremendous loss of life on all sides, impelled America and the Allies to shorten the war as soon as possible. Thus an atomic bomb was dropped on Hiroshima on 6th August, and a second bomb on Nagasaki on 9th August. On 8th August, after almost 6 years of peace, the Soviet Union declared war on Japan, and by 15th August the unconditional surrender of the Empire of Japan was announced, formally signed on 2nd September, 1945.

The Soviets invaded the puppet state of Manchukuo (Manchuria) on 3 fronts... from the north, so close to their own territory, from the east by sea, and also from the west, advancing over the mountains and deserts from Mongolia. Their army considerably outnumbered that of the Japanese army, and as the Soviets approached, many Japanese soldiers deserted. Others committed suicide. As their army retreated, many wounded soldiers were left to die on the battle field, whilst some Soviet soldiers committed 3 days of rape and pillage. Ordinary civilians of Japanese descent became stateless and homeless. Many were killed, others were taken off to Siberian prisons for 20 years, or escaped to the Japanese home islands where they were treated as foreigners. It was a truly terrible time, and the Sterns as unprotected women, would have felt very vulnerable in those early months.

With the Japanese vanquished and gone, both Margarethe and Susanne returned to school for the next 2 years. This involved attending the YMCA College in Harbin, situated in Novi Gorod (New City), some distance from where they lived, and reaching their destination was a daily challenge. The transport was an old Russian bus, with little fuel, and a kind of samovar at the back, filled with burning wood, presumably for the passengers' comfort. The bus would break down regularly en route, forcing the passengers to get out and push it, sometimes in extreme wintry weather...and also forcing them to confront some rather unpleasant Soviet soldiers, most of whom were more drunk than dangerous. The girls, by now, could speak fluent Russian, and with some maturity, careful not to incite them to anger, treated the soldiers like children, without serious incident.

As the curriculum at the YMCA was well-organised, in Russian and English, with the additional asset of high calibre teachers, Margarethe was inspired to make the most of her college time, appreciative of her chance to study, after working as a dressmaker for 2 years. Earning money was still a problem, so she continued with sewing at home in her free time. Her fellow students included three Jews, one White Russian, one Soviet Russian, one Czech and two Poles. Some of those expressed their antisemitism at the start of the academic year, but over the course of 2 years studying and interacting together, their prejudiced views changed; they realised that more united than divided them, and the group became very good friends.

For eight months Harbin was under the military regime of the Soviet Army who were intent on looting everything they could, including whole installations to send them back to the Soviet Union. Libraries were emptied, and during the winter there was no coal for heating and very little electricity. Daily living was tough.

Any societies or institutions that were non-communist were closed down, including two Zionist organisations, Betar and Maccabi, of which Margarethe was a member. It was at these Zionist meetings that she learned with horror about the Nazi genocide of the Jews in Europe, and about the deaths of her own relatives and friends who had remained in Germany. She would also have realised how justified her parents had been in fleeing Europe for China. The sudden and early death of her father, the responsibilities she assumed at a very young age during the privations of World War 2 and the hostilities in Manchuria, were definitely character forming, but caused her to grow up very quickly, without enjoying a carefree, teenage life.

Following the end of World War 2, the Chinese Civil War broke out in June 1946 for 3 years, between Mao Zedong's Communists and the Nationalists, led by Chiang Kai Shek. Nationalist personnel stationed in Harbin required a translator for one of their diplomats, from Russian to German, and Margarethe was offered the job. She was delighted, as the post was well paid and prestigious, more exciting than any of her previous work. She was encouraged to learn Chinese (Mandarin), but she had little time or application to take that really seriously.

Although the Nationalists initially showed greater strength in the conflict, they gradually lost out to the Communists who were supported by tens of thousands of starving Chinese peasants on the mainland. Additionally, the Red Army launched an invasion of Manchuria where they were given considerable assistance by the Soviet Union. In 1947-48, when the

Communists marched into Harbin, the Nationalist officials of Chiang Kai-Shek left the city. In October 1949, Mao Zedong proclaimed the People's Republic of China, with Beijing as its capital. About 2 million Nationalist Chinese who lost the war left mainland China for the Isle of Taiwan. Margarethe lost her well-paid job, and returned to dressmaking.

Chapter 9: Decisions

Although the Soviets closed down and liquidated the two Zionist organizations in Harbin, the Betar and Maccabi, the beautiful yacht, Kadima, belonging to Maccabi somehow escaped their attention, and that was where Margarethe and her Zionist friends, many of whom were German, would gather for their meetings, to make plans and disseminate information.

What was clear to the group was that following the end of World War 2, when first the Japanese and then the Chinese Nationalists had been defeated and thrown out, nobody wanted to live under either Soviet or Chinese Communism. When the Chinese red flags rolled into town, all evidence of the old culture or foreign influence was destroyed, from Confucius to American, English and German books, fiction or non-fiction. Volumes were piled into wheelbarrows, carried away and destroyed; even newspapers. All Chinese who worked for foreigners were encouraged to inform on their employers, and many businesses were confiscated.

Almost everyone of the Russian Community in Harbin, and certainly the Jews, were striving to leave, but these efforts were frustrated by an uncooperative Soviet Consulate. The German Jews all wanted to get out of China as soon as possible, but thanks to Adolf Hitler, they were stateless, and the only way to get out was through the Soviet Consulate. Each month, for nearly 2 years, one member of Margarethe's group went to the Consulate with a list of those desirous of leaving the country, but with no result. With great frustration, as the months passed, they gradually realised that the list on which their names were written had never left the Consulate. They were back where they started.

By 1948, Golda Meir had become Foreign Minister in Moscow, and therefore wielded considerable influence and authority in that position. Margarethe's Zionist group in Harbin wrote to her, enclosing the list of German emigrants, explaining their predicament of statelessness, and in her turn, Golda Meir sent back some kind of official identification for each of them. This provided them with the means to leave China, which was a blessed relief to them all, even though in 1939 the country had literally saved their lives.

Within the Stern family there was no unanimous agreement as to where they should spend their future years, since Marlene and Susanne had never been Zionists, and therefore were not particularly attracted to Palestine or what would become Israel. It was the unknown, and did not stimulate positive thoughts in them. For Margarethe, there was no indecision. She was proud to be Jewish, a member of a Zionist organisation, even if it had been liquidated, and she could think of no better place to spend her life than in the Jewish homeland, the newly established State of Israel. She wanted to belong, to live with those of similar aspirations and to play her part in the building up of a new democratic country...and she would never return to Germany. Potsdam, her city of birth, would shortly form part of the German Democratic Republic, behind the Iron Curtain.

A very special day for the Harbin Zionists was 14th May, 1948, the day of the establishment of the State of Israel, and many of them celebrated with great jubilation at the Sterns' home. With their visas or means to travel, the mixed group were free to leave China, but for Marlene, Margarethe and Susanne, a year had to pass before that would be possible. Firstly, they had to agree where to go, and consider all the risks of life in Israel which they took seriously. By that time the Arab-Israeli war had broken out which involved the Arab League...Egypt, Jordan, Iraq, Syria, Saudi Arabia and Lebanon; tremendous opposition, but with a victorious result for the Israelis. On a more domestic level, there would be no chance of taking the contents of their lovely home with them, so before departure, everything had to be sold or given away...all the furniture, library and pictures...which was hard for them all, but particularly for Marlene, since they contained such poignant memories of her married life.

At last in October 1949, the family was ready to leave for Israel, together with other German and Austrian Jews, some Poles and a few young Russians. The latter were lucky to be able to leave, unimpeded, since many others had been confronted with various bureaucratic obstacles to surmount, or fell for Soviet persuasion, and returned to the Soviet Union where they paid a very high price for having done so. Together with the other emigrants, the Sterns left Harbin and made their way to Tientsin, a journey of over 650 miles by train, to await a ship which would take them to Israel. In Tientsin, they were welcomed by the large Jewish community of that city who took care of them and provided them with accommodation for a whole month.

Margarethe and Susanne appreciated the sense of freedom there left by the American Army, and also the feeling of plenty, a contrast to the atmosphere engendered by the Red Army. During that waiting period, Marlene felt most unwell, perhaps the result of stress from the political upheaval and the wrench of leaving their home, to travel to the unknown.

At the beginning of November1949, the long awaited ship finally arrived, but it bore no resemblance to the luxurious Conte Biancamano of their previous voyage ten years earlier. Named the Wooster Victory, and built by the California Shipbuilding Corporation in Los Angeles in February 1945, it had been used in that year to transport American troops from France back home to the United States. In 1947, it was bought by the shipping magnate, Alexandre Vlasov, and used to transport Displaced Persons from Genoa to various parts of Australia and South Africa in August 1948, and subsequent similar voyages to Australia in that year. It was arranged through the United Nations, that on its return voyage, the vessel would sail to China to rescue Europeans who were fleeing the Communist forces, including many Jews and White Russians in Shanghai.

Comfortable cabins were replaced by 2 large dormitories, one for men and the other for women and children, with more than 200 people in each, providing virtually no privacy and plenty of noise. Since the Suez Canal was closed, the ship was forced to sail around the Cape of Good Hope where the crew and passengers encountered very rough seas for a number of days, and nearly everyone was seasick. Although the ship called at some of the ports they had passed on their way to China, it was forbidden to disembark, and that regulation was particularly frustrating at Cape Town where lots of Jews, bringing gifts, came to greet them at the quayside, but the passengers were still unable to get off the ship, even for a short time. On the whole, it was an unpleasant journey lasting 2 months during which Marlene, Margarethe and Susanne occupied themselves by looking after and entertaining the small children aboard.

When crossing the Mediterranean and Europe loomed into view, the ship first docked at Genoa where some of the emigrants wished to disembark to return to Germany and other parts of the continent, before it proceeded to Israel. In late December 1949, the Wooster Victory finally arrived in Haifa amid great excitement and delight to those on board. All the young people dressed in their best clothes, sang Zionist songs, and the Israeli flag which Margarethe had personally made and sewn was held proudly aloft. After years of waiting, and 2 months of anticipation aboard ship, they were about to make aliyah, and their cup overflowed with emotion.

Chapter 10: Israel

The excitement and joy of setting foot in Israel...the Promised Land...was only slightly dampened by the DDT shower given to each immigrant on arrival! From there all were directed to 'Shaar Aliyah Camp' for new immigrants, at the Receiving Centre near Haifa, where they waited in line to be registered, and where each was given a Jewish name. Marlene became Miriam, Susanne became Shoshana and Margarethe's name changed to Margalit.

The camp itself was built to hold 5,000 immigrants who were meant to stay for 4 or 5 days to undergo a medical examination, and then be assigned permanent places of residence in Israel, before being bussed to their new home, but it actually became impossible to evacuate the large number of immigrants before another ship or plane arrived, so many stayed in Shaar Aliyah for weeks or even months.

The next port of call was to Atlit, a coastal town located about 20 kilometres south of Haifa where the British had built a detention camp in the late 1930s to accommodate illegal immigrants. When the State of Israel was established in May 1948, it was used for processing and housing new immigrants, and comprised a series of Nissen huts. The newly-arrived were directed to these corrugated iron barracks, 50 to each hut, including men, women and children, not only from China, but from Iraq, Greece, Romania and Poland.

The winter of 1950 was one of the coldest on record, with snow falling even in Tel Aviv which was a rare event, and filled the young with awe and delight, but living in the Nissen huts proved a cold, spartan experience for the elderly, particularly when the roofs fell off in the storm. This situation meant they had to be transferred to other accommodation where the younger immigrants tried to make life tolerable for the elderly by hoisting up blankets between the beds to create more privacy. Fortunately, there was no shortage of food, although it was not to everyone's liking; unsurprising, since they hailed from several parts of the world.

The expectation at Atlit was to stay at least 3 months, and, in theory, by that time the new accommodation would be ready for each family, but nobody knew where these flats would be located. The new Israelis were allowed to leave the camp to visit relatives or go to Haifa or Tel Aviv, but forbidden to seek employment. Finding a job meant leaving the camp and forfeiting the flat or house.

Deprived of relatives in Harbin following the death of Jakob, and still mourning the murder of loved ones left behind in Germany during the war years, the Sterns were truly delighted to discover that they had family in Israel; relatives on Marlene's side who had made aliyah from Berlin in the 1930s. The Sachs family were living on a kibbutz, Ein Hashofet, in northern Israel, in the Hills of Ephraim, where in the early days the settlers had to defend themselves against armed attacks from Arab gangs on a nightly basis. Each day the division of labour was accepted and welcomed by the settlers, even though their professional lives in Berlin had been very different. They were now living the Zionist dream, and warmly received the recent additions to their family.

By Pesach (Passover) of 1950, Marlene and her 2 daughters were still living in Atlit with no immediate prospect of moving into a new home. When a friend of Marlene's invited them to a celebration of Pesach at her kibbutz, 'Ramat Yochanan', established in 1931 and some 25 kilometres from Haifa, they accepted with interest and enthusiasm. Margarethe was moved by the beauty of the religious service, and so attracted to the kibbutz way of life, that she decided to stay...for a whole year.

The advantages were obvious. After so much upheaval of leaving China, the unpleasant voyage to Israel and the discomfort of Atlit, daily life in the kibbutz, in contrast, was stable, secure and productive, with no worries of making ends meet, providing a daily opportunity of absorbing Hebrew, and making new friends some of whom were highly qualified, erudite people, content to work on the land and serve Israel. As well as taking her turn with chores, Margarethe toiled in the fields for several hours a day, producing flowers for export, mainly gladioli, gerberas (African daisies) and dahlias...which was a newly introduced facet to Israel's developing economy.

During that year, Marlene became companion to a wealthy, elderly lady living in Tel Aviv. Susanne joined a moshav in Kfar Daniel in central Israel, about 11 miles from Ramla, established by Mahalniks, that is, Jewish

World War 2 veterans from English speaking countries, on the lands of a de-populated Palestinian village. There are some differences between moshavim and kibbutzim. All property on a kibbutz is communally owned, and can include factories as well as farms, whereas on a moshav the property is individually owned, although the farming implements are shared.

As much as Margarethe valued her year at Ramat Yochanan, and was encouraged to stay and to study, she could not envisage living forever on a kibbutz. The choices were few. Since she was unmarried, her decision to leave Ramat Yochanan meant two years' national service in the army. She expected the experience to be frightening or nerve-wracking, but it proved to be worthwhile and satisfying, so that the 2 years passed very quickly. After her basic training, she was directed to headquarters, and assigned to a job in an intelligence unit, utilising her knowledge of 3 languages, German, Russian and English. The work colleagues and friends she made in the unit tended to speak English all the time which did little to improve her knowledge of Hebrew.

After leaving the army, short of money and determined to become independent as soon as possible, Margarethe enrolled in a course of paediatric nursing, organised by the Women's International Zionist Organisation (WIZO) which in Israel provided a tremendous service to immigrant women. After 18 months' training, which apart from the medical knowledge she gained also improved her command of Hebrew, she was offered a job in their department for premature babies where she stayed for nearly 3 years, deriving great satisfaction from the work, and gaining the independence she craved. At first, she could just about afford to share a small flat with an army friend, but gradually her accommodation prospects improved, when another friend invited her to share a larger flat and its expenses.

In Israel, reserve army service was mandatory,(and to a less extent still is), understandable in the 1950s when the country was surrounded by hostile Arab nations intent on her destruction. In those early days, reserve service amounted to about one month each year, sometimes more, and a large part of the Israeli population served in the IDF reserves. They were used to receiving special call-up letters sent to the reservists' postal address, telling them when and where to attend.

It was on reserve army service that Margarethe met her future husband, Josef Taglicht, who was known as Joe to all his friends. Like Margarethe, Joe was born in Germany, the only child of Berish and Sara Taglicht who were originally from Lodz in Poland, and rented a knitwear shop in Berlin. Joe, as a youngster of 12, recalled the terrifying occasion in 1938 when two Gestapo officers took his father away at night, with just his hat, coat and passport, and expelled him back to Poland. Joe never saw his father again. Almost as traumatic was Kristallnacht, when the windows of Sara's shop were shattered, the merchandise thrown out onto the street and looted. Like Marlene, she was forced to clear up the debris, and personally pay for the damage, before she was able to join her husband in Lodz.

Sara had to think quickly to preserve the life of her son, and had heard of Kindertransport. She contacted relatives in London, Mark and Eva Raphael, begging them to invite Joe to England, to provide him with a home, and sponsor him with a guarantee that he would not fall burden on the British government. The Raphaels, of course, accepted, and in May 1939, Joe was able to join 300 other German Jewish children travelling by ship from Hamburg to Harwich, and by train to London, where on arrival they were assigned to homes and schools. Much later, Joe discovered that his parents had died in Auschwitz, and this information was recorded at Yad Vashem in Jerusalem. But for his mother's courageous decision, Joe would almost certainly have become a death statistic too.

Joe's war years were very different from those of Margarethe. During term-time, he and another Kindertransport boy of similar age, were boarded and educated without charge by Christians who ran a school in Acton, London, but when the Blitz started, the school was moved out of London to Henley-on-Thames, in Oxfordshire. Joe spent the holidays with the Raphaels and their 2 children, Roger and Jane, who lived in St John's Wood.

Despite being immersed in an unfamiliar environment whilst at school, and suffering terribly from home sickness, Joe proved himself to be a brilliant scholar, and went on to attend the Cathedral Boarding School in Hereford, though not as a choral scholar. On the strength of his academic achievements, he was admitted on scholarship to Cambridge University to read English at the age of 16.

In the 1950s, he emigrated to Israel, served in the army and later met Margarethe. They married in Jerusalem in 1956, lived happily together, and Margarethe continued to work for WIZO until she got pregnant. They went on to raise 3 sons...Yuval, Danny and Rafi. After returning to the UK for 2 years with his growing family, Joe gained his D.Phil in Old and Middle English at Oxford University in 1960, and became a professor at the Hebrew University of Jerusalem where he remained until his retirement.

The Holocaust and the establishment of the State of Israel had brought Margarethe and Joe together, and also many other couples, each with an individual story to tell, and with love and hope in their hearts to try to build a better world.

Epilogue

In company with many surviving European Jews of her generation, Margarethe's life has not been free of pain and trouble. In her childhood, she encountered the most virulent and violent form of antisemitism, witnessed the depressive effect it had on the adults close to her and took part in the necessary escape of her immediate family to China to save their lives. Whilst still a child, she tragically lost her father, and was forced to abandon her education, albeit temporarily, to work and to provide extra income for the family. After World War 2, she mourned the loss of numerous, loving relatives and friends in the Holocaust...in fact, almost anyone she knew who was Jewish and was left behind in Germany to the non-existent mercy of the Nazis.

She has known what it is to live in an unsafe and volatile environment in Shanghai, in Harbin with the Japanese occupation, followed by the Soviet invasion with its hardships, the Chinese Revolution and the establishment of Chinese communism. Later, in Israel, working on the land, in the army and as a nurse, she struggled to become solvent and independent, with no prosperous parent to sort out her difficulties. Together with all Israelis, she has suffered from the unnerving threats and effects of war, suicide bombers, missiles and intifadas. In 1976, she and Joe, lost their first born son, Yuval, in a tragic accident whilst serving in the Israel Defence Force, and in 2005, she lost her beloved husband, Joe.

These days, as a proud Israeli, her view of life is positive, informed and outward-looking, and it is easy to detect a twinkling of humour and laughter in her eyes. There is no bitterness. Her enjoyment of people, literature, learning and music is ongoing. She has been a loving and ethical role model to her sons, of whom she is rightly proud, to her daughters-in-law and grandsons, and is at her happiest in their company.

Marlene Stern, Margarethe's mother, on her doorstep in Harbin, Manchuria

Margarethe Stern, aged 21

The whole Stern family on the Sungary river

Arriving with flag on boat to Israel

Susanne, Margarethe and Marlene in Harbin

The Stern children and friends on the Sungary river

CPSIA information can be obtained
at www.ICGtesting.com
Printed in the USA
BVHW031942171021
619162BV00006B/329